For Caroline,

For long friendships.

Armitage

i'm not sure about god

jesus is a different matter

BY WILLIAM ARMITAGE

Published by Words In The Works LLC
info@wordsintheworks.com   www.wordsintheworks.com

For Beatrice and Arthur.
Maybe you're listening.

You can't know, you can only believe
—or not.
—*C.S. Lewis*

Faith consists in believing when it is
beyond the power of reason to believe.

—*Voltaire*

I'm not sure about God.

Not the one I learned about in Sunday School anyway.

I know there's a force in my life and heart that's greater than me.

Something that gives me strength and courage. Something to hold on to.

I have no doubt about that.

But if it's not God, then what?

A Higher Power of my own choosing?

The Universe?

Guardian Angels?

The forces of Mother Nature?

Maybe it's *my* mum who died in 1984 and whose presence I still feel every day.

Many years ago, I met a man named Arthur. He lived in London's East End. I had never laid eyes on him in my life before that Saturday morning at my niece's house in Forest Gate.

He told me we were destined to meet.

Then he told me things about myself that only I knew.

He told me things that would happen to me and they did.

He told me my mum was standing next to me, watching out for me, and described her perfectly, right down to the grey streak that ran through her hair.

He had never met her either.

What's more, she had been dead for over ten years at that point.

I asked him how he knew so much about me

and he said without further explanation: "It's what I do."

I should have been freaked out. But for some reason, I wasn't. I've often wondered whether Arthur was God. Or that God appeared in the form of Arthur because he wanted to speak to me directly.

I was at a pretty low point in my life then. The sadness of a divorce I didn't want. Feeling estranged from my children. Battling the alcoholism I wouldn't admit to. I remember distinctly saying to my sister: I am so unhappy.

I talked to Arthur a couple of times on the phone after that. I told him I'd like to write his story but he said no. Then we lost touch. Or maybe we haven't. Maybe Arthur is watching over my shoulder all these years later as I type the introduction to this book.

Arthur changed something in me.

It was at that point I segued from writing advertising copy to writing personal essays that made me happy.

I wrote about my childhood.

I wrote about the joy I felt when I went to Sunday School at the London City Mission.

Mr. Phipps was the minister and Mrs. Phipps played the piano. I loved the choruses we sang: *"In my heart there rings a melody..."*

I wrote about the day I was awarded a New Testament Bible for memorizing verses.

John 3.16.

For God so loved the world, that he gave his only begotten Son. That whosever believeth in him...

And I do.

I believe there was a man named Jesus who lived two thousand years ago and who walked from town to town in what we now refer to as the Middle East.

I guess it follows that if I'm not sure about God, then I'm not sure that Jesus was the Son of God.

I know I don't believe this man named Jesus had otherworldly gifts.

I don't believe he could turn water into wine. Or that he could raise people from the dead. Or that he could heal people just by touching them.

As far as the miracles are concerned, I like to read between the lines on those as you'll see later in this book when I talk about *The Five Loaves and Two Fishes*.

Although not miracle performing, I do believe that Jesus had a special gift. Or rather, he gave them.

He gave the gift of kindness.

And compassion.

And generosity of spirit.

He looked out for the downtrodden. He felt the rich could do more for the poor.

He preached gratitude. Being thankful for the things we have instead of wishing for things that we don't.

He taught us humility. How not to overate our

own importance.

He taught love—a gift we could *all* give if we wanted to.

These are perennial lessons, don't you think?

And look at the gift of all those great expressions he gave us that we still use today: *He thinks he can walk on bloody water!*

If he really told them as documented, I think his parables were brilliant insights. They also show how little the world has changed.

In the parable of *The Hidden Treasure*, Jesus explains how little *real* happiness there is in worldly possessions. Try telling that to a world where we have to have everything and have it instantly. *Priority shipping only!*

Here's the thing about the miracles and what you can take away by reading between the lines—by not taking everything in the Bible literally.

Let's talk about the Resurrection for a moment. So what if Jesus didn't *actually* rise up on Easter morning?

His resurrection is real nonetheless. He came back from the dead in a sense, didn't he?

Look, two thousand plus years later, we're still talking about him. He is as alive today in people's minds (and hopefully, hearts and actions) as he was back then.

Just like my mum is alive in my heart and mind and the hearts and minds of all my brothers and sisters.

And it's not just life after death. It's love after death.

Especially if you live like Jesus did. Putting others before yourself. Trying to see the good in people. Not rushing to judgement because someone is different from you.

Yes, I know, we've heard all that stuff before. And naturally we say, YES! That's how I live.

But do we?

I took a Methodist Lay Speaker course in 2011. I got my certificate. And I preached for about a year. Taking the pulpit when the minister was on vacation or simply taking a break. I went to other churches to help out when there was a need for a preacher to step in. The story of how all that came about comes later in this book.

I stopped preaching mainly because the church I was assigned to seemed to care more about filling the pews than fulfilling the needs of the neighborhood.

There were people within a few blocks of the church that could have used a bit of comfort. Some company. Errands run. A warm meal.

One day, I found loads of tins and packages of food that had been donated during a food drive. They had sat in a little used room in the church hall long after their expiration date because no one had bothered to distribute them.

The tins and packages of food had been forgotten about. Just like the people who could have used them most had been forgotten about.

Then there was a change of church leadership at the district level. Our one pastor was replaced by a group of pastors with rotating duties. We would have different preachers each week.

Even though I was having my differences with our pastor over the way we served the local community, he was a good person.

And he gave us the sense of comfort, continuity, and familiarity that I believe a congregation looks for in their pastor; one trusted person to go to with their troubles, their spiritual questions, and in my case, even their disagreements.

I became really disillusioned.

I joined a church with a good outreach program and a pastor (just the one!) I liked a lot, but where my lay speaker qualifications wouldn't allow me to preach.

It didn't matter.

Delivering food on Thanksgiving morning to the sick and housebound was a better use of my time. I think that man named Jesus would probably have approved.

Even with my doubts about God, I love going to church.

I try to arrive early. I like watching the pews fill up. I love listening to the choir warming up. I love the singing. And even though I am tone deaf, I love belting out the hymns from my childhood.

"Praise him! Praise him!"

John Wesley, founder of the Methodist Church, wrote directions for singing. I take them to heart every time I'm in church.

He wrote: Sing lustily and with good courage. Beware of singing as if you were half dead, or half asleep; but lift up your voice with strength.

"To Thee with heart and mouth I sing."

John Wesley should know about singing. He and his brother, Charles, published fifty-six collections of hymns over five decades. Charles alone wrote an astonishing 8,989 hymns.

Regardless of where I stand with God, hymns

move me. Literally bringing tears to my eyes.

As the writer, Tom Ehrich, once said, who can fail to be moved by *"How Great Thou Art."*

Look at the passion in these words:

And when I think of God,
His son not sparing,
Sent Him to die,
I scarce can take it in;
That on the cross,
my burden gladly bearing
He bled and died
to take away my sin.

There was one occasion though, when a hymn moved me to tears and I was troubled by it.

It wasn't until weeks later that I seemed to understand why.

It was a Sunday late in 2014 and the choir at the Presbyterian church I had started attending sang *"In the Garden"* as the chorale offering that day.

I had heard the hymn before of course, but it

wasn't one I counted as a favorite. As they sang—it was a lovely arrangement—I suddenly was aware that tears were streaming down. A lump came to my throat. But there wasn't the usual awe or joy in these tears.

Instead, I was agitated. Unsettled.

And that uneasiness stayed with me all day. I even called a minister friend the next morning to chat about the experience.

In February 2015, my sister died.

Only she and her husband had known the seriousness of her illness until the very end—she was always a very private person and never wanted to worry others.

I later learned that her illness had been diagnosed late in 2014. Right around the time I had been upset by the hymn in church that Sunday.

My brother-in-law asked me to speak at the funeral. I flew to England.

The opening hymn my nieces had picked was

"*In the Garden.*"

I had forgotten until that moment, until seeing the order of service, that the hymn might not have been my favorite but it *was* my sister's.

I gave the eulogy. Just barely.

The gathering of our family afterwards was a wonderful experience. We are a large family, living great distances from each other, and don't get together often.

It was like a final gift from my sister.

I eventually returned to America on a Saturday in March. I went to church the next morning.

The opening hymn was "*In the Garden.*"

The great Brazilian writer, Paulo Coelho, said: "Every human being should know two languages; the language of society and the language of signs. One serves to communicate with other people, the other serves to understand God's messages."

I can't help thinking to this day: If only I had

understood the sign that previous year—that that hymn *"In the Garden"* was telling me something. I might have got to my sister's side before she died.

*

Meeting Arthur changed me; my sister's passing changed me yet again.

Her death underscored my rebirth.

I had been sober five years at that point.

I had been given a second chance at life.

And at her funeral in a beautiful Norman church deep in the Sussex countryside, it was my sister's words from the letters and emails we had exchanged over the years, as I read them aloud to the gathered family and friends, that brought the awakening that I really *was* truly happy with the few things I had; the sobriety I had achieved. I didn't need or want much of anything else.

"There are so many times recently," my sister wrote to me on one occasion, *"when I have*

walked into a store and said, 'What am I doing here? There is absolutely NOTHING I need.'"

She went on to say:

"David and I have all that we need in each other. I have never been rich, but I am blessed with a loving partner."

Then she added:

"I have also been given the gift of obtaining joy from such simple things."

She wrote me a note after I had wished her happy birthday.

"Thanks, William…having a lovely day…blue skies, sunshine, lambs jumping in the fields next to our house…and David's love. Who could want more?"

Who *could* want more?

But we do, don't we?

We want it to go on forever.

I was holding on to my belief in the God of my Sunday School and lay ministry course so I could hold on to the belief that I would earn a place in heaven.

But by the time I had finished reading my sister's eulogy, I had set aside any internal debate (and fears) about an afterlife.

I decided from that moment on, to live in full what I would later call my *'life after.'*

Which brought me back to Jesus and *not* God.

That meant living *this* life—my life on earth—in a better way.

Caring for and being useful to others.

Enjoying the here and now.

And I reckon after I've done that, I'll just go to sleep. Then get a bit more sleep. And a bit more after that.

Now, what about coincidences?

We've all had those moments. You know, you think about someone, the phone rings, and by golly, it's that person!

It's almost a cliché.

Again, Paulo Coelho has something to say about coincidences that appeals to me more.

"Coincidence is the language of the stars. For something to happen, so many forces have to be put in action. When you see signs or coincidences, the Universe is talking to you."

I believe that.

And sometimes the Universe has a more meaningful reward in store than hearing from a person you were just thinking about.

Here's a very special example.

I had drink with a talented photographer friend in New York City before heading off for a summer vacation in Newport, Rhode Island.

My friend was looking for a title for a speech she was going to give about her work—how one thing in her career led to another. As if planned, but not actually by her. We discussed calling the speech, *The Threads of Life*.

When I told her I was on the way to Newport, she said, "You must visit Vernon Court. It's a beautiful old mansion on Bellevue Avenue dating from 1900. It now houses the American Museum of Illustration. It has amazing art. But in 1963, it opened as an all-girls college and that's where I went to school."

I told her I would visit for sure. I would even

take pictures for her.

In the car on my way to Newport, I started singing, *"We're all going on a summer holiday..."*

Summer Holiday was the lead song from the 1963 film of the same title starring a beloved English singer by the name of Cliff Richards.

I wasn't sure why that corny old song suddenly popped into my head but you know how songs do sometimes. And after all, I was going on vacation!

After a few days on the beach in Newport, I decided I would visit Vernon Court. It was closed.

The second time I was halfway there and *Summer Holiday* popped back into my head.

I thought about the blue skies and sparkling seas depicted in the film and decided the weather was way too beautiful to be inside a museum that day. I went for a long walk along the clifftops instead.

Then my vacation took over and I forgot all about Vernon Court.

Two days before I was due back in New York City, I got an email from my photographer friend. It wasn't specifically addressed to me but was a general reminder to her friends about an upcoming gallery opening of her latest work. But it did in turn remind me about Vernon Court and the museum.

I decided to give it another try. Third time lucky. Vernon Court was open.

It is indeed, as my friend told me, a lovely old mansion with wonderful works by Norman Rockwell, Howard Pyle, Maxfield Parrish and so many more great American illustrators.

I was in the Maxfield Parrish room and had a question about one of the paintings. I looked around for someone who might work there and be able to help me.

There was a beautiful, elegant woman standing by the doorway. From her posture;

she was standing with a very straight back, the thought immediately crossed my mind that she might have once been a dancer.

I spoke to her and asked my question about Maxfield Parrish.

"You're English," she said after a few minutes chatting.

"And so are you," I replied.

"Actually, I'm Australian. But I moved to England when I was quite young. To dance."

I was surprised—her English accent was very refined. I wasn't surprised by the dancing part of course.

"Yes, I had you pegged for a dancer. What kind of dancing?"

"Ballet. Then I moved into films and television."

"Any films I would know?" I asked.

"Do you remember Cliff Richards? And *Summer Holiday*? That was one of the films I was in."

This time I was astounded.

Bowled over.

"You're not going to believe this," I began, "but that song has popped into my head a couple of times over the last several days. Once when I was actually on my way here."

We had an immediate rapport. An *Ecstasy of Connection* as I read in a poem once. Especially with our mutual English background.

And now we are going into our second year together. As a couple.

And here's the thing. If I had continued to the museum the second time I tried to visit, she wouldn't have been there. She later told me she hadn't been working that day.

Now, don't tell me all that was a mere coincidence.

It was *The Threads of Life* at work.

Thank you, Universe/my mum/Arthur/God, and my photographer friend, for the signs that led me to the most beautiful love imaginable.

*

I like praying.

Who am I praying to if I'm not so sure about God?

Well, I guess to that "force in my life that's greater than me."

Praying is meditation for me. A quiet moment at the end of each day when I can hear myself.

I don't ask for things. Not material things anyway. I don't ask for better luck. Or more money. Or for Tottenham Hotspurs to win the Premier League.

I ask only for clarity.

If I'm experiencing a difficulty, I ask to understand why.

If I feel I could have done better as a person in some situation or other, I ask to be shown the way.

I also make a point of listing the things I was grateful for that day.

Do my prayers get answered?

Sometimes.

Sometimes I believe I am talked to in ways I just don't understand.

I recently was in discussion to write a series of illustrated books for children.

Without knowing quite what the subject matter was, I put in a proposal simply because I liked the artist's work. Something in the email he had written to me also connected on a level that seemed more than just business.

I sent off my proposal.

That night my girlfriend and I watched *Shadowlands*—the film starring Anthony Hopkins and Debra Winger that examined the life of the English writer, C.S. Lewis, during the time of his marriage to Joy Davidman.

We were so moved by the film, that we sat up late reading more about Lewis's life and books. I learned things about his books on Christianity that I hadn't known before.

That night, I prayed for clarity on three

different writing projects that had fortunately come my way over the past several days. I knew I couldn't do them all in the time frame, so which one was right for me? I said I was grateful for the opportunity to bid on them all regardless of the outcome.

Early the next morning while I was researching C.S. Lewis quotes—literally while I was reading and filing them away for possible use in this book—an email came through from the artist I had sent the proposal to the afternoon before.

He too had felt a connection. And then he went on to say:

"Before we proceed any further, you should know that this is a Christian book. You might not be comfortable with the subject matter. But if you are, you'll understand when I say I want the books to speak to children the way the books of C.S. Lewis did."

Now again, that's too weird to call it just a mere coincidence.

My girlfriend had been trying to get me to watch *Shadowlands* for weeks but it was that night we watched it; the very day I had been contacted about that particular children's book series—one that invoked the works of C.S. Lewis.

Was that my prayer being answered?

Was it Arthur again?

Or my mum?

Or maybe even…God?

I don't know, but I expect to start work on that book series any day now.

God moves in a mysterious way.

Incidentally, people think that phrase is from the Bible. It's a common misconception. It's actually from a popular English hymn written by William Cowper in 1773.

But talking of mysterious ways.

I find pennies.

A lot of people do of course. If you google "What does finding pennies mean?" you'll see loads of answers.

Finding a penny means variously:

It's a message from someone you love who has passed on.

The Angels are watching out for you.

Great fortunes are heading your way.

Heads up, it's lucky. Tails up, not so much.

And so on.

I like a story I heard some years ago.

A very wealthy man pulled up in his Rolls Royce to a fancy restaurant. He was going to have dinner with a friend. As he climbed out, he spotted a penny on the sidewalk. He bent down and picked it up.

His friend laughed, and said: "Don't you have enough money without the need to pick up a penny?"

The wealthy man turned the penny heads up in his hand.

"It's not just a penny. It's a message. What does that say?"

"In God we trust," said his friend.

"I might be wealthy but that doesn't mean I'm without worries. I've been concerned about something all day long. When I find pennies, it's almost always when something is on my mind. I believe it's a message from God. Telling me to simply trust."

After I heard that story, I started finding pennies.

First it was just on the sidewalk. Or a parking lot. Where you might expect to find them.

And then something strange happened.

They started turning up when something was on my mind. A worry. A concern. Money. Work. A decision I had to make.

What's more, they started turning up in unlikely places.

On a table when I know there wasn't one there moments before. Or sitting there on a shelf in a cupboard I had opened just a little while earlier.

Then it got stranger.

Just when I was thinking I hadn't found a penny for a long time, one would turn up. Within minutes of me thinking about it. Sometimes, seconds.

You're probably thinking I've gone off my rocker.

But I tell you, it's true.

I have quite a collection of pennies that I've found over the years now.

Are they all a message from God?

I don't know. But here's the thing. In a funny way, I guess that God/The Universe/my mum/Arthur are all looking out for me.

If I ever run out of money, I'll just put all those pennies they *'might'* have sent me in a bag and cash them in at the nearest Coinstar machine.

Postscript in the "You can't make this up" department:

Less than an hour after writing the passage about finding pennies, I was standing in line at the supermarket checkout, editing and rewriting the passage in my mind. I looked down and there on the ground a few feet in front of me—heads side up—was a penny.

And I kid you not—there's absolutely no writer's embellishment here—it was glinting in the sunlight.

*

I only put together a handful of sermons.

Although I mostly followed the Lectionary—a weekly, pre-selected collection of readings from the Bible that preachers and churches use as a worship calendar—my words didn't always stem strictly from Biblical roots.

My sermons were just chats really.

Short stories. Sharing thoughts. Sharing meditations I had read and liked.

I won't for a moment pretend to be some amazingly brilliant theologian with advanced philosophical interpretations of the *Word*.

I used sources and quoted other people a lot.

I welcomed the great suggestions of a couple of minister friends. I used and quoted passages from *Feasting on the Word*, a brilliant resource for preachers.

But my Sunday chats seemed to connect with people.

Someone suggested I should share them by publishing them.

Looking back on the sermons today, I obviously see a lot of references to the God I'm not so sure about now.

There are things in the following pages that might contradict my current viewpoint.

But I haven't changed the sermons.

They're printed here more or less as they were given, in a talking style for me to deliver to a congregation.

Which means they may not flow quite like a polished book manuscript but you'll catch the drift.

The passages or words that are *italicized* are

mainly quoting and highlighting the Bible text I was preaching from that day. I also used *italics* to identify hymn titles.

Wherever you stand with God, or the idea of a God, I hope there's something in the following pages that might touch you in some way.

As I used to say to myself after devoting a good chunk of my week to working on them, the hours I spent on my sermons was all worthwhile if something connects—even if it's with just one person.

LOVE BY THE BASKETLOAD.

I was at the *Fancy Food Show* in Washington DC a few weeks ago. I was helping a client of mine exhibit a new range of salad dressing products.

The prospect of feeding (or least providing a taste of my client's product to) the expected 20,000 show attendees over a three-day period was pretty daunting.

But like the parable of the mustard seed, we found a little goes a long way.

We discovered a loaf of bread could be cut

into one hundred small cubes to be dipped in little cups of the dressing. And that one jar of salad dressing made fifty miniature salads. Anyone who stopped by our table was served. And at the end of the three days, we found we had actually brought too much to the show. We had lots left over.

On a hillside in Galilee two thousand years ago, late in the evening, with no Pizza Hut or any other fast food chain to order in from, the disciples told Jesus there was nothing to feed the multitudes but five loaves and two fish.

And Jesus said: Bring what you have to me. He ordered the crowds to sit down and he looked to heaven and blessed the food. And then he broke the loaves.

Now this wasn't some magic ritual that would allow the bread to multiply itself.

This was an expression of praise and thanksgiving. Jesus acknowledging that God will provide. For all.

And maybe what happened next was the real miracle.

As the disciples went among the people with the broken pieces of bread, maybe the people didn't reach into the basket with its meager five loaves and two fish.

Maybe they reached into themselves.

In the wake of listening to Jesus that day, seeing his compassion for the sick and needy, they too put others first.

Trading in selfishness for self-sacrifice.

Maybe the first person reached into their own basket or bag and said, "You know what, I think I might have brought something with me. I'm sure I must have. Give the loaves and fish to someone else while I'm looking."

Or there might have been someone like my landlady who loves to feed and always cooks for ten even though there are only four of them. And maybe that person said, "Look, I've got plenty here, I can feed this whole group around me. Go ahead and move the baskets on."

And maybe there was someone like my mother who always pretended she was on a diet, because she wanted to make sure there was plenty for the rest of us first.

As the mealtime prayer says, *Make us ever mindful of the needs of others.*

Tom Ehrich said in a recent meditation, compassion begets compassion, love begets love, and a small loaf turns into abundance.

Abundant thinking means giving freely and easily to others.

That raises an important point in the text here. Jesus didn't say to the disciples, don't you worry about feeding them, I'll do it.

No, he said to the disciples: You give them something to eat.

He was reminding the disciples about the power they had to nourish others. The power we *all* have.

It's an inherent spirit of generosity—God

given. And we should use that power.

As AA's twelfth step says, what we have freely received, we should freely give.

And when we do, we will find that we are the recipients of something wonderful too.

A friend of mine has been actively involved in the Midnight Run in New York City for many years. The youth groups from her church along with many other organizations, take food and clothes to the homeless in dark parts of Manhattan in the wee hours.

I asked her what the reaction of the homeless was to these gifts.

"Oh, they appreciate it of course, but the kids are the ones getting the real gift. Seeing another side of life. Understanding that the sick and needy should not be forgotten."

I don't think there's any question that those kids come back from the Midnight Run with their personal baskets fuller than when they left.

And all ate and were filled; and they took up

*what was left over of the broken pieces, twelve
baskets full.*

At the end of the final day of the *Fancy Food
Show*, I noticed teams of enthusiastic men,
women, and teenagers in crisp white shirts,
volunteers as I later found out, pushing trolleys
around the food aisles.

The backs of their shirts were printed with the
words: Food Recovery.

I stopped a couple of the young men and
asked them about their work.

"We take all the food that's left over from the
show and give it to the needy," they said.

"How many will you feed?" I asked.

"Not sure," one of the young men replied.
"But we expect to gather up 100,000 pounds of
food and we won't sleep now until it's all been
given out."

That was the inherent spirit of generosity at
work.

Love by the basketload.

Can we look at our own lives and ask: Do we give more than we take?

Share more than we hoard?

Help more than we hurt?

Love more than we hate?

And even in times of great personal need, instead of focusing on what we don't have, can we focus on what we do have and give thanks for that?

Do you remember when they used to serve food on airplanes?

There's a well-known story about Parker Palmer, the Quaker theologian and philosopher. Many years ago, he was a passenger on a plane that pulled away from the gate at an airport in the Midwest. It taxied to a remote corner of the field and stopped.

You know the feeling: the plane stops and you look out the window and see that you're not on the runway and the engines wind down and your heart sinks. The pilot came on the intercom and said, "I have some bad news and some really bad news. The bad news is there's a storm front in the west, Denver is socked in and shut down. We've looked at the alternatives and there are none, so we'll be staying here for a few hours. That's the bad news. The really bad news is that this is so unexpected we have no food on board and it will soon be lunch time."

Everybody groaned.

Some passengers started to complain, some became angry.

But then, Palmer said, one of the flight attendants did something amazing.

She stood up and took the intercom mic and said:

"We're really sorry folks. We didn't plan it this way and we really can't do much about it. And I know for some of you this is a big deal. Some of you are really hungry.

"Some of you may have a medical condition and really need lunch.

"Some of you may not care one way or the other and some of you are happy to skip lunch, so I'll tell you what we're going to do.

"I have a couple of breadbaskets up here and we're going to pass them around and I'm asking everybody to put something in the basket.

"Some of you may have brought a little snack along—something to tide you over—just in case something like this happened, some peanut butter crackers and candy bars.

"And some of you may have a few LifeSavers or chewing gum or even Rolaids.

"And if you don't have anything edible, you might have a picture of your children or spouse or girlfriend or boyfriend or a bookmark or a business card.

"Everybody put something in and then we'll reverse the process. We'll pass the baskets around again and everybody can take out what they need."

What happened next was amazing.

The griping stopped.

People started to root around in pockets and handbags, some got up and opened their suitcases stored in the overhead luggage racks and got out boxes of candy, a salami, even a bottle of wine.

People were laughing and talking.

She had transformed a group of people who were focused on need and deprivation into a community of sharing and celebration.

She had transformed scarcity into a kind of abundance.

After the flight, which eventually did proceed, Parker Palmer stopped on his way off the plane.

He said to the flight attendant, "Do you know there's a story in the Bible about what you did back there? It's about Jesus feeding a lot of people with very little food."

"Yes," she said. "I know that story. That's why I did what I did."

STAND UP. STAND UP.

There were two main bodies of water associated with my childhood. Where I learned to swim. And where I went swimming.

The first was a place called Southend.

Or *sowf*-fend as London's East Enders pronounced it. Southend was actually the estuary of the River Thames. But to us, Southend was the seaside. A kind of Cockney Coney Island.

You knew you were at the seaside because there was the sound of seagulls, a faint whiff of salt, boats, the world's longest pleasure pier, an amusement park, lots of fish and chip shops, seafront pubs, and fluffy pink candy floss. Or cotton candy as it's called in America.

And of course, the beach.

Not a soft sandy one.

It was mostly small stones and sharpish pebbles. But after the pavements and concrete of the East End, it was a beach to us all the same.

I had my first pair of swimming trunks. A swimsuit. I had been allowed to run around as God intended up to that point. Nylon was about to invade our world but the trunks my mother found on sale were made of wool. Bright red. When they got wet, they bubbled out and stretched and hung to your knees. I now believe they were designed to test your tolerance to painful rashes.

Mum and Dad rented deckchairs. They were just a couple of pennies for the day back then.

My older brothers and sisters spread out on

the sand. (Or what there was of it.) But I was desperate to get into the water to see if I could now swim.

I was convinced my new swimming trunks would bestow that ability upon me.

How's that for early faith?

My mother's faith in my swimming trunk's abilities wasn't quite so strong. She allowed me down to the edge of the water but to go in no farther than "just above your ankles."

As she walked back towards the others, I glanced over my shoulder to make sure she was there. I laid down in the few inches of water and made arm movements as if I were swimming.

I basically crawled along on my stomach.

Swimming on, not in, the water other people were just walking through.

I soon tired of this and all the people stepping over me, and decided to stand up. I pulled up the water-logged swimsuit to protect my modesty. Then I looked up and down. I suddenly realized I couldn't see my mother. Where was she? I started to panic. Searching out all the faces. I cried out. Suddenly mum was there beside me. With my towel. With the comforting cuddle only mums can give. Now she didn't quite say what Jesus said to Peter: *O thou of little faith, wherefore didst thou doubt?*

But it was words to that effect: "You silly sausage. You didn't have to worry. I was there the whole time."

As Jesus was. *Take heart, it is I; do not be afraid.*

The other body of water from my childhood was the local swimming pool. Very conveniently located opposite our church. As luck would have it, we had ninety minutes or so to kill between Bible study early Sunday morning and Sunday worship. We used that time to go swimming.

There was a Sunday when we studied the text in Matthew we've just read; Jesus walking on water. The swimming pool, of course, was the perfect place to bring the text to life.

Ignoring the "no running or shouting" signs, we backed up as far as we could from the edge of the pool and ran as fast as our legs would carry us. Singing "*Onward Christian Soldiers*" at the tops of our lungs, we leapt into the air, stiffened our backs, and tried to walk across the surface of the water. We got a step or two and then rather rapidly submerged.

But here's the thing.

We didn't know it then, but we were doing something important. We knew for sure of course, that we could walk (run!) on the solid tile surface around the edge of the pool, but seeing how far we could get walking on the water meant trying something we didn't know the actual outcome of.

We were, in a way, testing our faith.

And in order to deepen our faith we sometimes need to test it.

'Lord, if it is you, command me to come to you

on the water.' He said, 'Come.' So Peter got out of the boat, started walking on the water, and came towards Jesus.

Like the other disciples in the boat, Peter was panicked in Matthew's account by the sight of Jesus walking on the water. But Peter stepped out of the boat in faith and faithfulness. And there's another important point here. The effect one person's risk can have on a whole community. The effect Peter's faith in Jesus had on the other disciples in the boat.

When they got into the boat, the wind ceased. And those in the boat (The other disciples that is) *worshipped him* (Jesus), saying, *'Truly you are the Son of God.'*

At our Maundy Thursday supper back in April, we were sharing stories around the table in the fellowship room. And someone said, "I was with a group of people I didn't know a few days ago and as we were introducing ourselves to each other, I simply said my name and then added,

'I'm a Christian.' And I felt good about it. And I would have been totally okay if the people asked me more about it."

Do we take the risk of stepping out of our personal boats enough to say, "I'm a Christian?"

Being bold about our faith can make others bold about theirs. And help yet others who might be of *little faith*.

Now, I'm not suggesting we should run up and down the street with a bullhorn shouting "I'm a Christian! And if you don't believe me, come over to the lake this afternoon and watch me walk on water. Without the benefit of water skis and a noisy speedboat!"

No, I mean being bold by living truly with Christian values, acting in a *truly* Christian way. Being Christian and not being afraid to speak of it. Maybe simply mentioning to a fellow worker on a Monday morning that "church was great yesterday." Watch the reaction.

"Stand up, stand up for Jesus," says the old

hymn, *"Ye soldiers of the Cross."*

Now stepping out in faith is not a guarantee that we won't get caught up in troubled waters. Or have times of fear. Fear is such a prevalent part of our lives. Including fear of spiritual enthusiasm.

But the text has another important message for us here:

Jesus reached out his hand and caught him.

When we are willing to step out of our comfort zone, it can be risky. Fearful. But it's also exciting. It's what God calls us to do. With the assurance that Jesus will be there for us. When we need it most. And that's the big reward.

The Reverend Dr. William H. Willimon is the Bishop of The United Methodist Church in North Alabama.

He said in a sermon once: If Peter had not ventured forth, had not obeyed the call, he would not have had this great opportunity for recognition of Jesus and rescue by Jesus.

If we don't get out of the boat, if we only splash around in the shallow water, we'll never have the opportunity to test and strengthen our faith.

The second time I went in the water that day at Southend, mum came with me.

I waited at the water's edge while she waded out to waist high. She turned around, dropped down until only her head and shoulders were above water. She opened her arms and called me to her. I walked towards her, deeper into the water than I had ever been before. And then suddenly the water lifted me. I was swimming! Really swimming. Not wading in the shallows. And she was laughing.

Come on, says Jesus, joyfully, calling us to faith. Calling us to do his work. Do not be afraid, he says. Stand up. Step out of the boat.

OUR LOSS IS OUR GAIN.

I used to play football.

Now, this is not to be confused with the American game of the same name.

In my football, you do actually use your feet to move the ball around the playing field.

We call it "soccer" here in America.

I played on my church team, London City Mission United.

We held jumble sales in the church hall (rummage sales) to raise money to buy the team uniforms.

Our colors were light blue and dark blue. Our shorts came down below our knees. Our boots, up above our ankles.

The ball we played with back then didn't have the benefit of being plastic laminated.

We had to polish it with a special wax called Dubbin. To make it water resistant.

It never worked of course. One downpour, the wax washed off, and the leather became waterlogged. And extremely heavy.

If you tried heading the rain-soaked ball it was like banging your skull against a lead cannonball.

It often left you momentarily stunned.

But we loved our Saturday afternoon games. We were a good team. But we were never good enough to beat the Saint Ursula Rovers. The Wild Rovers as we called them after the song.

Saint Ursula's was the Catholic Church up the street. The team they fielded was composed of strapping Irish lads. They were the sons of construction workers and the local dockworkers. We believed their mothers fed them raw meat. And steel girders. For breakfast.

In other words, they were tough opposition.

We had the football brains. But they had the football brawn.

And so we went into each game, totally assured, that we were going to be killed.

Not *all day long* as it says in the text from Romans.

No, the valiant London City Mission United football team were going to killed just for the ninety minutes of playing time. But we were *accounted as sheep*. There was no question we were going to be slaughtered!

Our coach, David, was one of the church leaders.

He never lectured us after a Saint Ursula's game. No angry post-mortem. He was just there for us throughout. With extra quarters of refreshing orange to suck on at half-time. And after it was all over, he would always lower his voice, smile, and say, "They might have won again lads, but they have to get up for seven o'clock mass tomorrow morning." Our services didn't start until eleven.

We loved David. And he loved us. And he seemed to love us more when we played Saint Ursula's. Simply for turning up. For standing firm. Knowing that we would be playing at our own *peril*.

We weren't conquerors.

We were *more than conquerors*.

Because what mattered was that we faced the challenge. What we "won" was each other's love and admiration. Our loss on the field was our gain off it.

As I get older, I have come to realize, as many of us as do, that life can be a series of losses.

As we face hardships, distress, and perils, it's as if we are constantly dying a little.

Little deaths. Time and again. Where we feel

defenseless and crushed.

Sometimes our loss is self-inflicted. Simply because we don't get our priorities straight. I read a story of a man whose whole focus in life was his business.

Oh, he had a wife. And kids. But his main focus was his work. And even when he promised to make a ballgame, or recital, or a birthday party, there was always one more phone call, one more "quick" meeting to attend to that inevitably meant he wouldn't attend the one event he had promised his family. This man was struck by fatal illness at a relatively early age and as he lay gravely sick, he finally recognized all that he had lost. He had loved his business but his business couldn't love him back the way his wife and kids could.

A *New York Times* story told of a different family, the Sopers, whose Alabama home was devastated by the tornadoes.

"Losing Everything, Except What Really

Matters" read the headline.

And the story went on to tell how "Mr. Soper led a small army of power-saw-toting relatives and friends in clearing the jumble of fallen trees from his two-acre lot. He occasionally looked up to see his wife and his two children in their altered yard. His house nearly destroyed, he nevertheless felt blessed."

At the end of our lives, our relationships are all we've got.

Relationships, cared for, can give us a lifetime of love. Our relationship with God needs to be cared for too. Even though God's love is total and unconditional.

My mother died at a relatively young age. It was a terrible loss. I also felt a certain guilt. As Willie Nelson sang, maybe I didn't tell her I loved her quite as often as I should have.

But you know, her love for me never went away. Little things she said. Little things she did. Her words of wisdom. They've been with me always. Her basic goodness, kindness, and generosity of spirit—passed down to my own children. We have never been separated from her wonderful love. She lives on. Love after death.

Jesus said, *I will not leave you comfortless; I will come to you.*

Sometimes we forget about God and put too much expectation on human love alone, and we are devastated when it inevitably comes up short.

Spiritual writer, Henri Nouwen, described this as the difference between what he called the 'first love' and the 'second love'.

He wrote: The first love is from God, who loved us before we were born. The second love is from our parents, brothers, sisters, and friends, and it is only a reflection of that first love. Sometimes we expect from the second love what only the first love can give. Then we experience anguish.

When we come to God with humble, open hearts, we have room for the love that God longs to pour into us.

This is the love that we then pour out to others. And pour it we should. We are all God's ministers.

Beyond loved ones, the loss we talk about the most is the loss of financial security. And all the consequent losses that go with it. Loss of dignity. The loss of the ability to pay your bills on time. The loss of personal direction. And in moments of crisis, sometimes, the loss of faith.

I know a young man who lost his job.

Next came his apartment.

Then his health.

His very will to go on.

And he blamed God.

Why hadn't God answered his prayers? Why had God deserted him?

Why didn't God simply get him back all the things he had lost?

My heart went out to him. I wanted to tell him:

God doesn't cause our troubles. God is there to help us through our troubles.

Another friend spoke to him.

"You're not alone. We are all here for you. Whatever happens, you can totally rely on our love and care."

As the people of God, we are assured of God's all-encompassing love. And as the people of God, we are called to give that love as we stand beside the ones who are staring the likes of the Saint Ursula Rovers in the eye.

We are called to show up for each other. With the love that will not quit.

There is nowhere we can go that puts us out of the reach of God's love.

No dead spots as the mobile phone companies say in their ads. No loss of wireless signal. We have five bars at all times.

The message is clear.

For I am convinced that neither death, nor life,

nor angels, nor rulers, nor things present, nor things to come, nor powers, nor height, nor depth, nor anything else in all creation, will be able to separate us from the love of God in Christ Jesus our Lord.

CAN YOU HEAR ME NOW?

I woke up this past Christmas morning and did something I had never done before.

I decided to spend the whole of Christmas Day by myself.

My daughter lives in Sydney, Australia, so I knew she wouldn't be dropping by laden with presents for me.

My son had visited on Thanksgiving and wasn't coming down until the New Year.

Kind friends had invited me for dinner. But something inside wanted me to take the day for myself; for my thoughts alone.

I jumped on the 9:21 train into Manhattan; in time for the Christmas morning carol service at Saint Bart's on Park Avenue.

Now I love our church but every now and again, the magnificence and pageantry of worshiping in a great big, domed church like Saint Bart's is amazing. The several hundred seats were filled.

Afterwards, I headed over to 38th Street to attend an AA meeting at a group called *The Mustard Seed.*

I listened as people shared their hopes and fears and gratitude.

Then it was ice-skating in Bryant Park.

Just watching that is.

Citi Pond (that's C-I-T-I as in the bank) with its neon signs was not quite the bucolic version of skating in Manhattan depicted in the famous Currier and Ives print of 1862.

But nonetheless, it was fun to watch people

enjoying themselves so much in such a traditional Christmas way.

Back home, I lit candles, ate a simple meal, and read the stories of Jesus' birth from the gospels of Matthew and Luke.

Something, as far as I can remember, I had never actually done on Christmas Day itself before either.

Next morning was Sunday, my Boxing Day, and I came here to church.

Pastor Tom had started his well-deserved vacation and so we had a Lay Speaker.

I was intrigued.

I was familiar with preachers who stand in for pastors who are away.

I was familiar with the role of interim ministers.

But something connected with me. Lay Speaker. Back home, I googled in some keywords.

Within a click or two, up came: *Methodist Lay Speaking Course. Danbury, Connecticut.*

Classes start first week in January.

Now this was a pretty amazing sequence of coincidences.

First, I'm intrigued by lay speaking.

I google.

And then there's a course just a couple of towns over.

Starting the very next week.

But was I deliberately being led from one thing to another? By some force outside of myself?

A minister friend of mine always warns against magical thinking when it comes to God.

I couldn't help but wonder though…

God moves in a mysterious way as the old hymn says.

What I do know for sure is this.

In deliberately finding a quiet time over that Christmas holiday, I also found a place of peace. And serenity. And even welcome solitude.

A Christmas where I didn't say: Thank

goodness that's over with for another year!

I took the time for deep, contemplative prayer. I got out of my own way; stopped trying to be at the center of my own faith and carved out a quiet space to let God in.

And, resting in the presence of God, I was able to let my heart tell me what God wanted to say.

I heard what he wanted of me.

When we turn down the noise inside the house, we might just realize there's someone knocking at the front door.

Can you hear me now? As they used to say in the Verizon ads.

And I so took the lay speaking course. And I have found true joy in this way of being of service.

Today is the Sunday in church when we celebrate our role as a *collective* ministry. The People's Ministry. When we all take the pulpit.

And we are blessed in this church. Blessed

with those that have helped the church survive and thrive. Blessed with people that have so many different talents.

We have gifts that differ according to the grace given to us we heard earlier. That passage goes on to say:

If your gift is to encourage others, do it!

If it is contributing to the needs of others, give generously.

If God has given you leadership ability, take the responsibility seriously.

And if you have a gift for showing kindness to others, do it gladly.

True ambition, I read recently in AA's Big Book, *is the deep desire to live usefully and walk humbly under the grace of God.*

Do you remember the very special words we said together on World Communion Sunday?

Did you really think about what we were saying?

God. Ask much of us; expect much of us;

enable much by us; encourage many through us.

This is the work God wants of us. Of all us.

Take a look at the front of your bulletins. There's an important phrase there. It's there every week but we might sometimes pass it by. Pastor: Tom Smith. Ministers: All God's People.

Again. Remember, ours is a collective ministry.

The body is a unit, though it is made up of many parts; And though all its parts are many, they form one body. So it is with Christ.

Can you hear him now?

What does he want of…you?

"Softly and tenderly Jesus is calling. Calling…for you and for me."

WHY ME?

Do you know that song by Willie Nelson?

The Last Thing I Needed First Thing This Morning.

He was obviously having a *"why me?"* day when he wrote that one.

He got a past due notice, his alarm clock went off late, trash was left all over his driveway, he spilled his coffee, and then his girlfriend dumped him.

All in one morning!

Good Lord! you could be forgiven for saying.

It can be tough being a country singer.

It was even tougher being a prophet.

How would we have coped with being God's messenger around 600BC?

In the course of his lifetime, Jeremiah was attacked by his own brothers, beaten and put into the stocks, imprisoned by the king, threatened with death, and thrown into a tank of water and left to drown.

And that was only the half of it.

"So why?" he asked God, *"Why me? I proclaimed your message. Just as you commanded. And yet you let my enemies rain down on me."*

You can just imagine Jeremiah plunking himself down on the nearest rock and shouting, "It's just not fair."

Unlike Willie Nelson, he didn't exactly complain that someone—God—had walked out on him.

But he certainly implied that God had failed

him. Deceived him even.

"Truly, you are to me like a deceitful brook, like waters that fail."

Comparing God to a river, all dried up just when you need him most.

We all have bad days.

Where it seems to rain on everything we do.

We try to do right but it all goes wrong.

Our good intentions land up in the last place we intended.

Our friends let us down. Workmates don't seem to understand us.

And life's personal earthquakes choose that very moment to erupt.

Jeremiah lashed out at his enemies. And his friends. And we lash out. And we ask ourselves, and our God, why?

Why me?

Jeremiah went on to list all the good deeds that resulted in his "undeserved" tribulation and personal misfortune. He made it clear to God that he wasn't out there having a good old time of it all. Laughing and joking around.

I did not sit in the company of merrymakers, nor did I rejoice.

And he wasn't happy with the way God seemed to be rewarding him.

So why me?

Maybe it's more about the "me" than the "why."

Me. Me. Me.

Self-reflection is one thing. But sometimes we look so far inward that we forget to look outward.

Have you ever written a screenplay in your mind? You know the sort of thing.

Where you say to yourself: Hold on a second, I did this, this, and *that* for this person. So how come they're not doing this, this, and *that* for me? They didn't even say thank you. Where's *my* reward for all the good I did?

You might even go so far as to write some

dialogue too. So next time I see him, I'll say...listen you...

When our self-reflection becomes self-pity and self-centeredness we need to remember what Jesus prayed in Gethsemane. *Not what I want, Father, but what you want.*

As Christians, we turn our lives and our will over to God.

And then we do get something in return. The big reward. Because God's promise to Jeremiah is a promise to us all.

If you turn back, I will take you back. I will make you a fortified wall of bronze.

They will fight against you, but they shall not prevail over you.

I will give you the strength God is saying. Not just to endure any given "mess of the day." Whether it's spilling the coffee or something much greater that has brought you to your knees. But the strength to survive the mess. Better still, with God beside you, right there in the midst of it, the struggle might actually bring out your best.

Your low point might well become the transition, the conduit to your highpoint.

Sometimes we need a difficult descent to climb more readily back up the ladder of life.

Sometimes by falling low, we learn lessons we might not otherwise have learned. We see life from a different viewpoint. A different perspective.

And we recognize just how precious life is. How short. And how all we really have, as a friend of mine said in a letter to me once, *is the grace and beauty of the moment.*

And as we try to move from this place of "why me?" we have to remember that others might still be stuck there. And we shouldn't rush to judgment about it.

Many years ago, my brother was dating a girl he was crazy about.

He was only nineteen or so and was madly in

love with her. There was joy and delight in his first true love.

But they were young. And their first love was just that. The first. And it ended. And he went through terrible despair and terrible pain and suffering when she left him.

In our house at dinner one night, my father said, "It'll be all right." And my brother, still in his agony, said something to the effect, "What do you know?" And both were offended.

My father and brother didn't speak to each other for weeks and weeks.

And then the pain and suffering became my mother's.

We lived in a tiny house in the East End of London and to have two grown men not speaking to each other under one small roof was just unbearable for her.

Live in harmony with one another, we heard from Romans. *Live peaceably.*

I remember the day my father and brother

reconciled. It was a day so many of us remember.

November 22nd, 1963.

The day President Kennedy was killed.

My father was watching the news on our black and white telly and my brother came into the room. For the first time in many months, one of them didn't immediately walk out. They watched together and shook they heads in disbelief and chatted together about it.

And I look at it now and realize:

In a moment where the entire world was overcome with pain and suffering, my mother had found joy and delight.

Yes, she was sad about the president. But all she cared about at that moment, was that father and son were speaking to each other again.

In our own lives, sometimes we need to listen quietly. When our loved ones are in pain, recognize that they may say things that are hurtful. Let them get it out.

Just as God let Jeremiah vent.

Recognize the moment for what it is. Don't take offense at it. And then move on. With no prejudice or judgment. With forgiveness in our hearts. And encouragement for them to go out again.

Just as there is pain and suffering there is also joy and delight.

Just as there is agony, there is ecstasy.

"Your words were found, and I ate them, and your words became to me a joy and the delight of my heart."

So, let's ask ourselves that question again, why me?

But let's do it from a different viewpoint. Let's not lament, but lift up.

When we are led by gratefulness and optimism and enthusiasm and hope, the wallowing "why me?" becomes the *wondrous* "why me?"

Why me? What have I done to be so blessed?

Wow. How fortunate am I?

I don't care what I don't have, look at what I do have!

For I am with you to save you and deliver you, says the Lord.

We are *all* blessed with God's warm embrace.

Why me? Why us?

Why not? says God.

INTER-DEPENDENCE DAY.

Independence Day has always been a bit of a challenge for me. Tomorrow, I will hang my Union Jack on the side of my house just as I have every Fourth of July since I came to America.

As you probably know, Union Jack is the nickname for the British flag.

I hang my Union Jack each year just in case the colonies are taken back; so the Realm will know I'm still one of them. Well sort of.

The outcome of the American Revolution was of course, that the brave colonials who took up arms, led America into an independent state; out from under the "yoke" of British Rule as the history books tell us.

But this isn't the *yoke* that Jesus is talking about in Matthew.

It's not the yoke of servitude.

Jesus is talking about the yoke of oneness. A yoke that binds us together in faith.

Making us inter-dependent.

Farmers used to yoke the young ox with the old experienced ox to train them.

Using a long piece of wood, carved to fit across the backs of the animals, the old ox took the major load with the young ox walking alongside him and learning from him.

The yoke Jesus asks us to share is comfortable. Lined with love.

Jesus—tied to those who are exhausted, weary, and burdened from carrying the load by themselves.

Jesus right there with us, walking with us,

teaching us and strengthening us side by side.

I remember an occasion walking hand in hand with my father in the countryside. I was full of questions. What's this, Dad? What's that, Dad? Why can't we go that way, Dad? And then of course the inevitable question, are we there yet, Dad?

And on the final walk back to the bus-stop to take the double-decker bus back home, my dad took all the load. With my body across his back. My arms around his neck. My legs holding on around his waist. My head resting on the back of his neck. Tired but happy.

Have you noticed how a certain kind of tiredness gives you a certain kind of happiness?

Working in the garden springs to mind; back aching but stopping to admire the clean flowerbeds.

The exhaustion that sets in after painting a room and putting the furniture back in. But then a glow comes over you.

The satisfaction of unpacking the final box of books after moving house.

Weariness is different.

It's not a satisfied tiredness.

And it tends to come from futile work.

Doing things that don't really matter. Worrying over things that aren't important.

My yoke is easy, and my burden is light.

Jesus' message here is simple. And full of promise.

The easy yoke means doing things with a purpose. Summoning forth your best. Being motivated by passion.

Attach yourself to me, Jesus is saying. Learn from me. Live out my mission in your own lives.

And you will find that living the message is easy. You will find joy in ministry.

I read that when we share the rich rewards of God's grace through our actions, when we integrate our faith into our daily lives, we are living out our possibilities and not our shortcomings.

Now of course, burdens don't just vanish. God doesn't wave a magic wand.

But no one should have to carry a load by themselves either.

As they say:

A problem shared is a problem halved.

Many hands make light work. Or at least, lighter work.

Lifting another's burden is sometimes as easy as simply holding a door open for a person who is weighed down with bags.

At the train station, helping a mother down the steps with a stroller.

At the supermarket, not burdening the person who only has one item to wait behind you while you check out a cartload.

Being aware of the needs of people around you.

Other burdens aren't as easy to manage.

The burden of addiction. The burden of

poverty. The burden of unemployment. The burden of anxieties and illnesses. And as we get older, the burden of worrying about whether we will become a burden ourselves in our twilight years.

These burdens are real. They need to be tended to. And we can help by simply being there for each other.

I love our community. This network. People I rely on. And hopefully who feel they can rely on me. We're tied together. Yoked in the best possible way.

There's the joining together but sometimes we also have to let go.

And remove the burdens we don't need to carry or even *realize* we're carrying.

A simple apology for our wrongdoing might be all it takes. A phone call to help make amends.

Letting go of a relationship that's simply wound down without letting go of all the good things about it; not letting any resentments diminish all the positive ways the relationship enriched your life.

I wrote a letter to my children this week and apologized for some of the harsh realities that affected their lives after their mother and I divorced. It wasn't easy, but I felt a burden lifted.

Sometimes we yoke ourselves to material things.

The all-consuming desire for success and honors.

Bigger. Better. More.

And what is success?

Is it seeing how many people you can climb over on the way to the top of the corporate ladder?

Or is it simply getting through a month and being able to pay rent for the next month?

Is success simply about living our lives with realistic expectations of ourselves, matching what we have to what we really need?

Maybe we shouldn't put too much of a *burden* on our friendships either.

If we take away some of the conditions we put around friendships, we might find we're left with a better friendship altogether; a friendship that isn't burdened by constant need and attention and demands but one that offers simple rest and comfort and the occasional kind word that means so much.

And that can be enough.

I have lunch with a friend every Friday. We know each other's strengths and weaknesses.

We don't overplay our roles in each other's lives. But we rely on each other. We depend on each other for our health and welfare.

I had to cancel our lunch last week. I cancelled again this past Friday.

He stopped by my house unexpectedly yesterday.

He lives twenty-five minutes away. So he wasn't exactly in the neighborhood.

It has become unusual for more than a week to go by without us seeing each other.

He was simply checking in on me.

This is the love, and compassion, and kindness Jesus taught.

The people-serving, sharing and sacrifice that will put the *'rest'* and *'peace'* in our lives.

What friends we have when we're yoked to each other through God.

"What a friend we have in Jesus."

ONGOING CONSTRUCTION.

Do you know what Westchester Potatoes are?

They come in all shapes and sizes. Big ones. Small ones. Round. Flat. Heavy. Light. Sturdy. Delicate.

It's the name farmers in these parts used for the stones and rocks that they dug up from their fields while they were plowing—readying the soil for sowing with real potatoes and other crops.

The stones were put off to one side of the field. They were laid in neat lines as the farmer continued to plow up and down.

Eventually these would become the beautiful rock walls you still sometimes see around here, the walls that helped the farmer divide up his land.

The neighboring farms did the same. And the fields that divided their properties were defined by a joint rock wall, a property line that they both built. A community wall.

These were the stones that were unwanted in the fields. *Stumbled over. Rejected.* But not *abandoned.*

They became *living stones.* Living with a new purpose.

Stones that look very much like these were used to build our church.

We've been through a lot of rebuilding lately, haven't we?

Our church has been renewed and restored and come alive. Look around.

It's beautiful. And we all love it. People have

worked really hard to get it to this wonderful place.

It is truly a defining moment in our history.

But now…after the new floors have been laid. After the new burners installed. After the walls have been painted. After the worn rugs have been replaced, the work of spiritual building continues.

We are the stones *inside* our church.

The *living stones*.

We come together not as a random pile of rocks strewn across the fields, but as stones belonging to a structure built on Jesus Christ.

We are called to be a community in God, stones fitting together as unified faith.

It's you and me and Pastor Tom and the people who came before us, and the people who will come after us; it's us together that are the true sacred places and spaces.

A temple made with our hearts, not with our hands.

The solid underpinnings that prepare us to serve others.

"We are the church. The church is a people."

In this ongoing construction, Christ is both our cornerstone and spiritual foundation.

Now we might ask: Is our building work solid so far? Have we skimped on the cement? Have we used sub-standard materials?

In other words, are we trying to live as Christ taught us? Are we doing the right thing?

As we know from our Sunday School songs, the foolish man built his house upon the sand.

But the wise man, well, the wise man built his house upon the rock.

He built it on the ways of Jesus.

Now take a look into the four corners of the church.

Where the walls come together is a place we don't normally spend much time.

But sometimes it's good to look deep into the corners of our lives.

Even if we don't always like what we see there.

It's where we tend to throw the things we don't want to deal with.

Things about ourselves we'd rather not face.

We'll take care of that later, we say. And later is always later still.

And these things pile up. Around us. And upon us.

These are the stones that we stumble over. But God is there to help us. He will bring us *out of the darkness* of the corner and *into his marvelous light.*

Sometimes there are people in those corners too.

People we love. But have treated badly.

People we have overlooked. Forgotten about.

Someone who wrote to us, made a phone call, enquiring after us, maybe needing our help.

But somehow, we never got back to them.

Just too busy, we justify. Simply not enough

hours in the day, we say.

We need to be there for those people. Because the day will come when we want them, need them, to be there for us.

Just as Jesus is there for us, day in, day out.

A pastor friend of mine recently visited a woman who suffers from agoraphobia. This woman had led a long and distinguished public career. But in retirement was struck down with this awful fear of leaving her home.

She can't get to the physical church. But she reeled off a list of all the members of the congregation who visit her. One person, one living stone at a time, the church has come to her. Her physical isolation, as dreadful as it is, hasn't become spiritual isolation.

In John, we heard...*In my Father's house there are many dwelling places. If it were not so, would I have told you that I go to prepare a place for you?*

We didn't have many dwelling places in my

house growing up; I lived in what was known as a three-up, two down. Three bedrooms upstairs, a sitting room come dining room downstairs and a small kitchen.

And there were ten of us. My eldest brother, poor man, slept on the sofa for years.

But you know, the house never seemed crowded.

Somehow, we all fitted in. There was room for us all.

And the room in our mum's heart was enormous.

She had a way of loving us all equally but making us feel individually special.

We lived in a pretty tough neighborhood and frequently heard family arguments drifting in from other houses late at night.

Mum used to tell us that life was too short to be angry at each other. She told us to love easily, to be kind always, to open our hearts to all.

My grandmother would visit. While Mum

played the piano, Granny would hoist her skirt daringly to her knee, do a little jig and sing *"Rich or poor, knock on the door and make yourself at home."*

I think God probably sings that song too.

Now, what about those other stones? The ones that come with a big stick.

Sticks and stones, they say, will break your bones, but names will never hurt you.

And yet name calling is so often a violent weapon in itself.

We sometimes say things that are hurtful. We act out of anger. We're sensitive people but we hurt other sensitive people with our carelessness.

Racism lives.

Chauvinism in all its senses lives. Elements of our society are looked down upon.

There are people whose quest for some semblance of dignity never ends.

The writer Tom Ehrich said in a recent column:

The first disciples were nothings, too. Jews in a Roman Empire, men and women of little status, followers of a blasphemer, living together in ways that violated cultural norms.

He goes on to say...then the Risen Christ came to them, breathed on them, fed them, commissioned them, and declared them a people, beloved of God and worthy. All of them: women and men alike, young and old, foolish and wise. All of them now belonging to each other and to God.

Once we were no people, now we belong to each other and to God.

No longer that random pile of rocks strewn across the fields.

I was once shown a very good use for a small stone like this.

My friend held it in his hand when he prayed at night.

And then he slipped it in one of the shoes he'd be wearing the next day. If he didn't start his day with another prayer and just pulled on his shoes, he was quickly and painfully reminded of the fact.

"What can I tell you?" he said as he rolled the stone around in his hand and spoke from his heart. "I'm a flawed human being just trying to be the person I believe God wants me to be. I shouldn't need a stone in my shoe to remind me to pray, I shouldn't need reminding that I'm trying to live my life as a Christian, but sometimes I do."

Sometimes we all do.

Amen.

The Closing Hymn
IN THE GARDEN

I come to the garden alone,
While the dew is still on the roses,
And the voice I hear falling on my ear
The Son of God discloses.

Refrain:
And He walks with me, and He talks with me,
And He tells me I am His own;
And the joy we share as we tarry there,
None other has ever known.

He speaks, and the sound of His voice
Is so sweet the birds hush their singing,
And the melody that He gave to me
Within my heart is ringing.

I'd stay in the garden with Him,
Though the night around me be falling,
But He bids me go; through the voice of woe
His voice to me is calling.

–Charles A. Miles. 1913

I've added some thoughts to a Benediction a friend
of mine used to give and that I have always loved.
I decided it would be a good way to close this book.

Life is short.

And all we really have is the grace and beauty

of the moment—not to be squandered.

So be quick to love.

Make haste to be kind.

Be willing to forgive.

Gladden the hearts of those you journey with.

And be grateful for all your blessings always.

Excerpt from:

Hymns I Want at My Funeral
—In case I go before telling you

I've enjoyed amazing grace all my life.

I'm just not sure I want it played at my funeral.

The hymn that is.

I guess if someone insists on it behind my back on the day there won't be much I can do about it.

But it is a bit of cliché now, don't you think?

Don't get me wrong.

Amazing Grace is lovely. It has brought tears to my eyes at many a funeral.

And I seem to be going to them with increasing frequency these days.

My friends keep dying.

Everyone I know now seems to be someone *I knew.*

The other day my girlfriend asked me to help her sync up her address book from her iPhone to her new MacBook. She decided to update it as well.

I was deleting while she was going through a battered old Filofax (remember those?) that she keeps as a backup in case technology lets her down.

"Dead. Dead. Dead. Kicked it. Popped her clogs. Wait! Go back to 'R' and delete Sybil Robinson. Poor old bugger—she went last July, bless her."

"You might not need an address book soon," I told my sweet friend who was now in tears.

Laughing.

Coming early 2018
(Hopefully it will be done before I am.)

hymns
i want
at
my
funeral

in case I go before telling you

BY WILLIAM ARMITAGE

ABOUT THE AUTHOR

William Armitage was an award-winning advertising copywriter before turning to the book marketing, editing, and publishing world. He is a Certified Methodist Lay Speaker. *I'm not sure about God* is his first book.

Made in the USA
Middletown, DE
17 March 2018